Canary Islands Travel Guide

Holiday Guide To Tenerife, Gran Canaria & Lanzarote

Christopher White

Copyright © Astute Press, 2012

All Rights Reserved.

No part of this publication may be reproduced, stored in a retrieval system, or transmitted, in any form or by any means without the prior written permission of the publisher, nor be otherwise circulated in any form of binding or cover other than that in which it is published and without similar condition being imposed on the subsequent purchaser.

If there are any errors or omissions in copyright acknowledgements the publisher will be pleased to insert the appropriate acknowledgement in any subsequent printing of this publication.

Picture Credits: © Astute Press

ISBN: 1480121614

Although we have taken all reasonable care in researching this book we make no warranty about the accuracy or completeness of its content and disclaim all liability arising from its use.

Table of Contents

Tenerife ... 6
Culture ... 8
Orientation/Location ... 10
Climate and When to Visit ... 11

Tenerife Sightseeing Highlights ... 14
Teide National Park ... 14
Loro Parque Zoo ... 16
Icod de los Vinos ... 17
Beaches ... 19
Masca Valley ... 20
Guimar Pyramids ... 21
Siam Park ... 22
Lago Martianez ... 24
Las Montanas de Anaga ... 25
Cliffs of the Giants ... 26

Recommendations for the Budget Traveler to Tenerife ... 28
Places to Stay ... 28
Places to Eat & Drink ... 31
Places to Shop ... 33

Gran Canaria ... 36
Culture ... 37

Location & Orientation 38
Climate & When to Visit 39

Gran Canaria Sightseeing Highlights 41
Las Palmas 41
Playa de las Canteras, Las Palmas 44
Vegueta, Las Palmas 45
Triana, Las Palmas 47
Maspalomas 48
Aqualand, Maspalomas 49
Playa del Ingles 50
Carnival, Gran Canaria 51
Teror 54
La Cumbre 54
Palmitos Park 56
Puerto de Mogan 56
Sioux City, Bahia Feliz 57

Recommendations for the Budget Traveler to Gran Canaria 59
Places to Stay 59
Places to Eat & Drink 63
Places to Shop 65

Lanzarote 68
Culture 69
Orientation/Location 71
Climate and When to Visit 71

Lanzarote Sightseeing Highlights 74
Arrecife 74

Timanfaya National Park ... 77
Carnival ... 78
Cueva de los Verdes ... 79
Wine Museum of Lanzarote ... 81
Beaches ... 82
Museum of International and Contemporary Art ... 84
Jardin de Cactus ... 85
Surf School ... 86
Lively Lady Show Bar ... 88

Recommendations for the Budget Traveler to Lanzarote ... 91
Places to Stay ... 91
Places to Eat & Drink ... 93
Places to Shop ... 95

Tenerife

The largest and most populous of the Canary Islands, Tenerife is a hotspot of rich culture, delicious food, fascinating history, and stunning natural wonders. Roughly five million tourists make their way to Tenerife every year, making it one of the most beloved vacation spots in Spain.

On the southwest end of the island, bustling resorts and upscale shopping options abound--the ideal vacation spot for the modern traveler looking for night-life and culture. After strolling the streets and shops, you can enjoy a meal and a drink in one of the many open-air restaurants, or dance the night away to music played by an international DJ in one of the large discos.

If you prefer nature's finery, Tenerife will not disappoint. The mountainous interior of the island and the green north remain much as it has during the last 500 years, and many of the unique species of flora and fauna that live there can't be found anywhere else in the world.

The Canary Islands also have some of the best beaches in the world, and Tenerife's 350 km of coastline offer everything from black pebble beaches and golden sand bays and tranquil water to rocky promontories with stunning views. Ask your accommodations about whale and dolphin-watching excursions and scuba diving rentals--both are popular in Tenerife.

And of course, visitors won't ever forget the drama of the volcanic landscape. Hiking paths are available through both eerie moonscapes and lush greenery. At 3,718 m, Pico del Teide is Spain's tallest mountain peak, and the intense colors of the surrounding lava formations make it one of the most breathtaking natural wonders in the world.

Tenerife's rich history can be explored in various museums and at several archeological sites. From the ancient pyramids of the north to the colonial churches of the south, history lovers will thrill at all the island has to offer.

Tenerife Sunset, Costa Adeje

Culture

The ancient Guanche people settled Tenerife around the first or second century BCE, and although the tribes no longer exist, evidence of their influence can still be found in place names and the local lingo of the island. Spain conquered the island in 1493, and the Spanish influence can be seen in everything from the food to the architecture.

Today, Spanish is the main language spoken by the island's 908,000 inhabitants. Although the island is officially a part of Spain, the vocabulary and pronunciation is closer to Latin American Spanish than Castilian Spanish. English, German, and Italian are also commonly spoken in larger cities.

The majority of people on Tenerife are Roman Catholic, and religion plays a large part in daily life and holiday festivities. Pilgrimages, or "romerias," are the most common festivities on the island, with citizens gathering to honor a local patron saint.

The people of Tenerife--known colloquially as Tenefenos--are warm, friendly and relaxed. Many of them are proud of the ancient Guanche blood that runs in their veins. Tenerife has been a melting pot of cultures for many years, but it still manages to retain its own unique identity.

But ancient history isn't the only thing that matters on Tenerife--the island is also a center of art and science, with twelve major museums, and several important educational institutions. The Astrophysics Institute of the Canaries even has an observatory located at the volcanic peak of Teide.

And visitors of every palate will find something to satisfy their taste buds in Tenerife. While mostly Spanish in nature, the cuisine of the island has been influenced by the many other cultures that have come and gone over the years in Tenerife. Seafood is popular fare, due to the island's location and easy access to fish and other sea life.

Some food items unique to Tenerife and the Canary Islands include "Canarian wrinkly potatoes" (potatoes that are kept in their skins, then boiled with salt), "mojos" (a sauce that comes in various flavors and textures), and gofio (cereal grains that are roasted and then ground).

Tenerife

Los Cristianos & Playa de las Americas

Orientation & Location

Tenerife is located near the center of the Canary Island archipelago, in between the islands of Gran Canaria and La Gomera. It sits roughly 360 km west of the coast of Morocco in Africa, and a little over 1200 km to the southwest of Spain, between 28° and 29° N and the 16° and 17° meridian.

Tenerife is the largest of the Canary Islands, with a surface area of 2034 sq km. The island was formed by volcanic activity approximately 20-50 million years ago, and the island has experienced eruptions as recently as 1909.

The island's highest point, Mount Teide, is the third largest volcano in the world, with a base at the bottom of the sea and a peak at 3718m above sea level. It is the highest point in Spain, and the tenth highest island worldwide. Because of the large changes in elevation, the landscapes and ecosystems of the island are extremely varied.

Climate & When to Visit

The balmy weather of Tenerife makes it an ideal vacation spot 356 days a year. But you may wish to plan your vacation around the high tourist seasons or one of the many festivals held throughout

Tenerife

the year.

From November to March, visitors from Germany and England escape the colder climates of their native countries in Tenerife, and these few months are considered "high season," despite a brief rainy season in November. The summer holidays are also busy, from May to August.

Tourists can find reasonable flights year-round, but the best bargains can usually be found from September to December and from March to May. Spring is one of the quietest times on the island of Tenerife, and if you're looking to avoid the bustle, this is the best time to visit.

Midsummer's Eve in June is celebrated with bonfires and beach parties throughout the island. Fiestas go on all month in July, celebrating the patron saint of the island. And of course, Carnival is one of the biggest parties in the islands, usually falling sometime in February or March. The Canary Islands have some of the biggest Carnival celebrations outside of Rio in Brazil.

Canary Islands Travel Guide

Mount Teide

Tenerife Sightseeing Highlights

Teide National Park

The 190 sq km park is home to stunning views, unique landscapes, and flora and fauna not found anywhere else in the world. A visit to the area is a must for any traveler coming to Tenerife.

One of the most spectacular things about this park is its unique variety of lava formations. Smooth *pahoehoe* lava, eroded badlands, and volcanic pipes and cones can all be seen throughout the park, creating an eerie lunar landscape, so much so that parts of Star Wars and the James Bond movies were filmed here!

The central point of the park is the stratovolcano, Mout Teide. The island's highest point, it is the third largest volcano in the world, with a base at the bottom of the sea and a peak at 3718m above sea level.

Canary Islands Travel Guide

There are several great ways to see the volcano itself, but one of the best is by teleferico, or cable car. The cost is 25 euros for adults, and 12.50 euros for children under 14, and the cable car runs daily from the visitor's center between 9 am and 4 pm, weather permitting. You can check the website for daily conditions.

Visitors can also take any of several footpaths that are available around the mountain. You need a special permit to climb to the very top, but even without the permit you can come close, and experienced hikers can make this 6-hour hike a day outing. You can call ahead to book a free guide, or explore on your own. Call 34 922 29 01 29 for more information.

There is a Visitor's Center at the park, where you can learn more about the geology of the area and obtain hiking maps. Conclude your day of exploration with a meal at the Visitor Center bar/restaurant, and stop buy the souvenir shop to grab something to remember your trip by.

Visitors should note that the high elevation also means greater variance in temperatures. In the winter, the landscape is covered in snow and temperatures are usually below freezing. During summer months, temperatures can reach above 40 degrees Celsius. Be sure to check weather conditions in the park before visiting.

Loro Parque Zoo

Located just outside of Puerto De La Cruz, this zoo is home to the world's largest collection of parrots. One of the zoo's special missions is to prevent the extinction of certain parrot breeds through protection and breeding, and today the zoo is home to over 3,000 birds from over 340 species. Be sure to stop by the "baby station," where baby birds are cared for into adulthood.

Other exotic animals are housed here as well, including tigers, gorillas, chimpanzees, and penguins. The penguin exhibit is especially noteworthy--Loro Parque has made a marvelous effort to recreate the Arctic, with 12 tons of artificially created snow falling in the exhibit every day. A glass panel runs alongside the water, giving visitors the chance to watch penguins both above the ground and underwater.

Loro Parque's mission is to rescue and protect animals from all over the world, especially from private owners who have attempted to keep wild animals illegally and mistreated them. At the Loro Parque zoo, animals aren't kept in cages, but in small versions of their natural habitats, making this zoo one of the best ways to see wild animals. There's also a subterranean aquarium with the world's longest submarine tunnel, giving tourists a chance to view some of the stunning sea life of the island.

The zoo also has the biggest dolphin show in Europe, which will delight visitors of all ages. Shows and presentations are also given daily at the penguin enclosure, the aquarium, the sea lion enclosure, the orca tank, and in the parrot area. And don't miss "Planet Life," a special documentary film made exclusively for Loro Parque, and shown several times a day in the park's Naturavision dome.

The zoo isn't too long of a walk from town, but you can also catch a ride on the free train that leaves every 20 minutes from Plaza Reyes Catolicos, outside McDonalds. Admission is 33 euros for adults, and 22 euros for children 6 to 11 years old. The zoo is open daily from 8:30 am to 6:45 pm, with the last entrance into the park at 4 pm. For more information on the park, visit http://www.loroparque.com/en/index.asp.

Icod de los Vinos

Located in the northwest corner of the island, this small town is home to a number of noteworthy sites, including several historical

Tenerife Sightseeing Highlights

churches and plazas, a volcanic cavity considered one of the largest in the world, and the ancient Dragon Tree. Situated on the coast, the town of 24,000 people is an idyllic and beautiful place to spend a day or two.

The Dragon Tree of Icod de los Vinos is one of Tenerife's most well-known attractions. Dragon trees are a type of plant native to the Canary Islands, Cape Verde, Madeira and western Morocco. Standing at 22 m high, the ancient dragon tree in Icod is reputed to have been standing for over a thousand years.

Although there is no definitive way to measure the tree's age (dragon trees don't have rings), most scientists believe the tree has been standing for between 600 and 800 years. The tree is located in a garden near the church of San Marcos, where visitors can sit and enjoy the view for free.

Icod de los Vinos' other main attraction is the Cueva del Viento, or Wind Cave. The cave is an underground complex of lava tubes, created by lava flows from Mount Teide's smaller sister volcano Pico Viejo around 27,000 years ago. The cave system is over 17 km long and has three different levels of passageways. Various geological formations can be seen in the caves, and fossils and other remains have been excavated. Guided tours are available through the caves four times a day, and cost 15 euros for adults and 5 euros for children, ages 5 to 14. More information can be found at http://cuevadelviento.net/inicio.php?id=eng&ix=1.

After exploring the caves and visiting the Dragon Tree, visitors can stroll through the town and take in its stunning architecture. Grand old homes border the Plaza de La Pila, and the 16th century church of San Marcos is worth visiting. The Icod Public Library has three branches that house the best cultural reference collections on the Canary Islands. After exploring the town, spread out a blanket on the sands in the sheltered bay of Playa de San Marcos to watch the sunset.

Beaches

The Canary Islands have some of the most beautiful beaches in the world, and Tenerife is no exception. Whether you're a beginning surfer looking for some waves to ride, or a sun-lover in search of some clean sand to spread out on, Tenerife won't disappoint.

All of the beaches listed here are "family friendly," but Tenerife also has many nude beaches. If you're not sure about a beach you'd like to visit, just check with your local accommodations or ask a local for a recommendation.

Las Galletas is a small fishing town with several small beaches that are great for beginning surfers. It was also a favorite of Jacque Cousteau, and the area has several great opportunities for scuba diving. Rental equipment is available, although you will need a license.

Torviscas is a popular beach on the Adeje Coast, and has various tourist activities and services available. This coast also has the beaches Torviscas and Fanabe, which are joined together by a long promenade, and have relatively calm waters that are great for swimming.

Two well-known holiday hotspots in the south include Playa de las Americas and Los Cristianos. Various sports and leisure activities are available in these tourist destinations. Water-sport enthusiasts will also love the laid-back southern beach of El Medano, which is home to the kite-surfing World Championship.

But the usually crowded southern coast does have a few quieter beaches. La Tejita is a golden sand beach located away from urban and populated areas. The water here is calm and not too deep, making it ideal for swimmers of all ages and abilities.

Las Teresitas is a golden sand beach located 7 km away from Santa Cruz. Dotted with palm trees, this beach is a favorite of tourists and locals. Showers, sun loungers, changing rooms, and food stands are all available.

Playa del Duque, next door to the popular 5-star hotel Gran Hotel Bahia del Duque, is one of the most luxurious beaches on the island. The fine grey sand slopes gently down into a swimming area, and sun beds and changing rooms are available for public use.

Be sure to leave valuables at home or under supervision while visiting the beach, especially during busy tourist seasons. Most beaches have restaurants and bars nearby, but you can also bring your own refreshments.

Masca Valley

Located near Mount Teide, the tiny town of Masca was once a pirate village, and until recently it was only accessible by foot or donkey. Now the town of 120 or so people is accessible by road, although be prepared for a hair-raising drive--the road twists and bends along the mountain face in a series hairpin turns. You can either rent a car and risk it on your own, or hire a taxi.

Once in the village of Masca, brave-hearted hikers can make the 7.5 km Masca Gorge Trek. The trail follows a streambed along a ravine, ending at Masca Bay. The hike isn't a demanding one as far as fitness goes, but there are some narrow areas that demand hikers to walk along a ledge above the stream, using a wire for safety. Visitors who suffer from vertigo or dislike hiking may not enjoy this hike.

When hiking Masca Gorge, be sure to take sufficient safety gear--most hikers recommend good shoes, water, a first aid kit, and thin gloves to help you maneuver over and around rocks. If you usually hike with poles, only bring one...you'll need at least one hand free. Do not attempt the trek after rain--the gentle stream floods easily, making the gorge extremely dangerous during rainfall. Also beware of falling rocks, and anticipate possible blockages. The hike takes between 3 and 5 hours, depending on conditions.

Various tours are available into the Masca Valley, with plenty of stops for photos and food. Be prepared to pay between 10 and 55 euros, depending on what the tour includes. The landscape is particularly breathtaking, and the unique flora and fauna you'll see in the area includes palms, buzzards, lizards, various mosses, and much more. The valley walls alternate between lush greenery and stunning volcanic rock. Most tours, car rentals, and taxis can be hired from the nearby city of Los Gigantes.

Guimar Pyramids

Located about 26 km away from Santa Cruz, the ethnographic park and pyramid site is a must-see for visitors to Tenerife. Research on the pyramids only began in the 1990s, so the attraction is a relatively recent site. The origins and age of these pyramids are still unknown, but many archeologists believe that the structures were built by the pre-Hispanic inhabitants of the island.

But the pyramids aren't the only things to see at this historic site. Visitors can explore ancient crafts and forms of transportation at the

Tenerife Sightseeing Highlights

"Early Navigation Tent." A full-size replica of Ra II, a modern boat made with papyrus and using ancient methods, is on display there as well. The original boat was built and used by ethnographer Thor Heyerdahl in 1970 to complete a cross-Atlantic voyage from Morocco to Barbados.

The site at Guimar also houses one of the world's largest photographic exhibitions of Easter Island. Life-size images line a route more than 100m long, and explain details about the legendary Moai and their famous statues. There is also a space that houses temporary exhibitions. An on-site restaurant and gift shop complete the appeal of the site.

There are several different tour options, ranging from 30 to 90 minutes, making this excursion a good half-day activity. The grounds also have spacious gardens with native plant species, and a playground for young visitors. Bring a lunch and enjoy the beauty of nature after exploring the pyramids.

To reach the pyramids from the north of the island, drive south on the TF-1 highway towards Playa de las Americas and take the Arafo exit at the 19-km point. If you're traveling from the south of the island, drive north on the TF-1 highway towards Santa Cruz and take the exit for Puertito de Guimar at the 23-km point.

The park and pyramids are open daily from 9:30 am to 6 pm, with the exception of December 25th and January 1st. Admission is 9.75 euros for adults, and 5 euros for children ages 9 to 12. An additional audio guide is available for 1.50 euros. Some of the additional exhibitions may cost extra. Call to learn about special discounts available for large groups. For more information on the pyramids, call 34 922 51 45 10, or visit http://www.abouttenerife.com/tenerife/pyramids.asp.

Siam Park

Located in Costa Adeje, this 46-acre Thai-themed water park has established itself as one of the best in Europe. Featuring various rides, pools, and slides, this park is sure to delight travelers young and old. Plan on spending at least a half day, if not a whole day, to fully appreciate the park.

Thrill seekers can get their fix at some of the park's rides. Crash along the waves in a family-size raft at Mekong Rapids or The Giant, or swirl around the edges of a thrilling whirlpool at the Volcano. Ride the Dragon, a twisting waterslide with a light-show inside its 20-meter funnel that lets you experience zero gravity for a few moments before plunging you into a pool at the end. The truly brave at heart can tackle the Tower of Power, a nearly vertical 28 m enclosed tube slide that passes through a surrounding shark and stingray tank before ending in a deep pool.

Visitors who prefer relaxation will love the Mai Tai Lazy River, the longest lazy river in the world. Float past lush vegetation and cascading waterfalls before ending at a Jacuzzi. You can also sunbathe or swim at Siam beach.

The Wave Palace boasts the highest waves of any wave tank in the world, at 3 m high. The park has an onsite surf school that uses the tank to teach lessons during certain hours. There is also a children's playground and various other slides and pools. The park has three restaurants and two bars, so refreshments are available onsite. Finally, the Floating Market transports you to a small shopping area where you can purchase souvenirs, snacks, and beach supplies.

The Siam Water Park is also the world's first "green" water park. Its water comes from the sea and is treated at an onsite desalination plant before being piped to the attractions. Afterwards, the water is recycled to healthily treat the park's plants. All energy comes from natural gas, specially chosen because of its low carbon emissions, and the park is currently working to increase its use of renewable energy.

The park schedule is subject to the weather, but generally the park is open daily from 10 am to 6 pm in the summer months (May to October) and from 10 am to 5 pm in the winter months (from November to April). Admission is 33 euros for adults, and 22 euros for children ages 3 to 11. For more information, visit http://www.siampark.net/en/.

Lago Martianez

Located in Puerto de la Cruz, this water park is a great and affordable way to cool off on a hot day. The swimming area is filled via the sea, and changes levels with the tide. The turquoise water is clean and warm. You can swim through various waterfalls and caves, with a large fountain featured in the middle of the main swimming area.

The water park has 8 pools, including kid and toddler pools, and a spa for visitors over 18. All of the pools are safe for children accompanied by an adult, as they aren't too deep. The lack of waves and depth make the pools perfect for swimmers of all abilities. Pool showers, bathroom facilities, and changing rooms are all provided.

Visitors aren't allowed to bring cooler bags or boxes into the facility, but there are plenty of places to buy meals, snacks, and drinks. There are also sun beds and sunshades available for rent. After swimming and sunbathing, duck into the new casino and try your luck at any of the machines or tables.

Originally designed by the Canary Island's famous artist/architect Cesar Manrique, the area around the pools is beautifully landscaped, with shady spots to get out of the sun and sculptures decorating the garden. Visitors should be sure to bring flip flops or pool shoes, since the ground between the pools is set with small pebbles and can be painful to walk on, especially when it's hot.

The park tends to be busier on weekends, so if you'd like to avoid the crowds, visit on a weekday. Admission is only 3 euros for adults, and 1.80 euros for children under 12. The park is open daily from 10 am to 6 pm from May to September, and from 10 am to 5 pm from October to April. For more information on the park, call 34 922 38 59 55.

Las Montanas de Anaga

Located on the northeast coast of Tenerife near Santa Cruz and La Laguna, these spectacular mountains provide a stunning look at the "Hidden Tenerife." The area consists of ravines, forests, coastline, and remote villages. Hiking paths and botanical gardens provide visitors with ways to enjoy the lush vegetation.

Formed by volcanic activity roughly 8 million years ago, this mountain range is one of the oldest parts of the island. Rainforests alternate with rocky cliffs from the mountain peaks down to the ocean, where hidden beaches can be found among rocky coves and forests.

Parque Rural de Anaga is an ecological park that was founded in 1987 to preserve and showcase some of the incredible biodiversity found in Tenerife. The Barranco de Las Huertas is another park providing amazing views over the craggy north coast of the island, in addition to showcasing some of the island's unusual plant life. The interesting rock formations of the Roques de Anaga are worth seeing as well. These natural Tenerife monuments in the sea have been shaped over millions of years by wind and water erosion.

Most of the hiking opportunities are challenging paths for the experienced outdoorsman or woman. If you are interested in hiking the area, be sure to check conditions with locals, research trails, and bring sufficient supplies. Don't attempt any of the hiking trails if you have health conditions that prevent rigorous physical activity.

Much of the Anaga Mountain area remains unexplored, and in some of the more remote villages, people continue the ancient Guanche tradition of living in caves. Because of their isolation, most don't have shopping or tourist attractions, but feel free to wander through and take in the sights and atmosphere.

If you rent a car and drive yourself, be sure to have a steady hand-- the roads consist of hairpin turns and sheer cliff faces. You can also hire a driver at one of the nearby cities--some offer excursions and tours to the area.

Cliffs of the Giants

Known locally as Los Gigantes, these sheer cliffs on the west coast tower above the sea at 500 to 800 meters high. The stunning view of these geological formations are so awe-inspiring that the ancient Guanches called them the "Wall of Hell" and believed they marked the end of the world.

The best way to see and fully appreciate these cliffs is by boat. A multitude of boats are available for hire in the small nearby port town of Los Gigantes. But the cliffs aren't the only attraction on these boat tours! Dolphin and whale sightings are frequent, and many boat excursions are billed specifically as dolphin watching trips.

Dolphin and whale watching boats leave from the port several times a day, and refreshments are usually provided onboard. The two main companies that provide tours are Nashiro Uno and Showgun. Nashiro Uno features glass-bottom boats, and can be reached at 34 922 86 19 18 for more information. Showgun can be reached at 34 922 79 80 44.

Time-tables and whale and dolphin sightings can't be guaranteed, but despite the small risk of not seeing any animals, the spectacular view of the cliffs makes the trip worth it. Be sure to bring your camera, although depending on the weather, you may need some protective casing to carry it in.

After seeing the cliffs from a distance and watching dolphins and whales playing in the waves, spend the rest of the day and evening in the charming town of Los Gigantes itself. A small black sand beach is the perfect place to sunbathe, and the quiet town is the perfect place to escape the noise and nightlife of the bigger resort towns. There are plenty of bars and restaurants, and a few evening amusements like karaoke.

Recommendations for the Budget Traveler to Tenerife

Places to Stay

Because one of Tenerife's reputation as a holiday spot, you're likely to find reasonable accommodations wherever you travel. Clean and friendly hotels are available for those not wishing to break the bank with their accommodation costs.

Although Tenerife is the largest of the Canary Islands, it's still fairly small, so even if you plan excursions throughout the island, it's possible to stay in one hotel for your entire trip if you wish. If you'd like to spend several days in an area before moving on, affordable accommodations can be found at various hotels and resorts throughout the island.

Hotel RF Astoria
Puerto de la Cruz
C/o Enrique Talg, 15, 38400 Puerto de la Cruz
34 922 38 46 89
from $27 - $67/night
Clean and friendly, this hotel is the perfect place to stay in Puerto de la Cruz. Well-stocked room kitchenettes include pots and pans and crockery, making it a great option if you'd like to avoid eating out every night. The outdoor swimming pool is small, but it stays warm throughout the year. Parking is available beneath the hotel for a small fee, or you can park somewhere nearby. A large supermarket and multiple restaurants and shops are all within walking distance.

Tenerfe Garden
Costa Adeje
Avda. Los Pueblos, 24, San Eugenio, 38660 Costa Adeje
34 922 71 55 24
http://www.tinerfegarden.com/main.html
from $31 - $79/night
Located on a hill near the beach, these basic apartments are a scenic place to call home during your stay in Tenerife. A large pool provides an area to lounge and swim on lazy days, and wireless internet access is provided throughout the entire hotel property. The reception desk is open 24 hours a day, and provides everything from car rentals to currency exchange. Be sure to ask about discounts they provide on excursions and tours to nearby areas of the island.

Mar Ola Park Apartments
Playa de las Americas
Avenida de Antonio Dominguez 18, 38660 Playa de las Americas
from $48 - $83/night

Recommendations for the Budget Traveler to Tenerife

Balcony suites with views are available for a reasonable price at this hotel, located near several shops and a supermarket. Kitchenettes provide guests with everything they need to enjoy meals in their rooms, but there's also a restaurant attached if you prefer to have someone else do the cooking. The spacious pool is cleaned every morning, and sun beds and parasols are available for loungers. The stunning beach Las Vistas is only a 15-minute walk from the hotel, and various bus-stops are nearby to take you all over the island.

Dragos del Sur
Puerto de Santiago
Av Maritima S/N, 38683 Puerto de Santiago
34 922 86 25 50
http://www.hoteles-losdragos.com/english/home.html
from $40 - $80/night
Stunning views of the craggy coast near Los Gigantes are provided from the hotel rooms at Dragos del Sur, and the apartments vary in size from 1 to 3-bedroom suites. The hotel also has rooms with wheelchair access, and the entire hotel is built with easy access for those with disabilities. The hotel has a bar and restaurant, and numerous other amenities for families and large groups. Various tours and excursions can be booked with the hotel reception desk, which is open 24 hours a day.

Hotel Santa Cruz Plaza
outside of Santa Cruz del Tenerife
c/Cruz Verde, 24, 38001 Santa Cruz del Tenerife
from $50 - $93/night
Located in a cosmopolitan area of Santa Cruz, this hotel is situated among shops, bars, and restaurants, making it the ideal place to stay while you explore the city. Many of the large and clean rooms either have balconies or full-length windows that can be opened to enjoy the view or to let the cool night breezes in. The hotel's restaurant provides a breakfast buffet with local as well as English breakfast items.

Visit the free shows in the Local 4 & 5-Star Hotels

Places to Eat & Drink

Tourism has brought culinary influences from all over the world, and there's no end to the variety of tastes. Here are some of the most highly recommended restaurants in various cities throughout Tenerife.

BAMBI Gourmet
Puerto de la Cruz
Calle Enrique Talg 15, 38440 Puerto de la Cruz
34 922 38 38 87

Recommendations for the Budget Traveler to Tenerife

http://www.bambi-gourmet.es/english/
$13 - $33
Ranked #1 of all restaurants in Tenerife, this vegan organic restaurant provides Romanian fusion that will leave you satisfied. Breakfast, lunch, and dinner are all available, as well as delivery and late night drinks. Walk-ins are welcome, but for guaranteed seats call ahead to make a reservation.

Carlos
Costa Adeje
Av Colon, cc. Club Atlantis, San Eugenio
34 634 70 31 33
$14 - $28
Seafood, Thai, and vegetarian options are the highlights of this international restaurant. Open for dinner only, starting at 6:30 pm nightly, this restaurant is the perfect place for a romantic dinner or late-night drinks. Seats fill up fast, so be sure to call ahead for a reservation.

CK's Bistro
Los Gigantes
Pasaje Jacaranda 2, 38683 Los Gigantes
34 616 22 67 77
http://www.cksbistrotenerife.com/
Sampling the local seafood is a must in the coastal towns of Tenerife, and this family restaurant in Los Gigantes is one of the best places to get it. Open for breakfast, lunch, dinner, and late-night dessert and drinks, you can stop by at any time of day to sample the local fare. Vegetarian options are also featured on the menu.

Oliver's Restaurant
Los Cristianos
Calle Andorra, Edif. Cerromar
34 680 69 39 77
$13 - $25

British fare is the main feature on the menu at this restaurant, and the atmosphere is perfect for families and special occasions. The generous portions make this an ideal meal stop for those dining on a budget. The friendly staff will make you feel welcome, and the food is superb. They are only open for dinner, so plan accordingly.

The Fisherman's Inn
Puerto de Santiago
Agustin Leon 31
34 922 86 24 91
This is one of the best places to sample local Spanish cuisine. Enjoy the stunning views of the nearby beach from the outdoor deck before eating lunch or dinner. Late night drinks are also available, but most visitors recommend stopping by just in time to watch the sunset.

Places to Shop

The Canary Islands enjoy a special Duty Free tax status, and cigarettes, alcohol, perfumes, and petrol are much cheaper in the islands than in the rest of the European Union. However, there are strict limits on how much you can bring into other EU countries. Be sure to check on item limits before attempting to travel back to the mainland with your goods.

There are also many electrical goods shops that sell cameras, video cameras, and other travel electronics. But be sure to ask a local or your hotel for a recommendation...not all of these shops are reputable! Many sell faulty equipment, and there are no warranties.

Also note that most shops follow traditional "siesta hours." The shopping day begins at around 9 am, Monday through Friday. Shops close for siesta during the hottest hours of the day, typically

Recommendations for the Budget Traveler to Tenerife

from around 1 pm to 4 or 5 pm, then reopen for another few hours, usually until 9 or 10 pm. Shopping hours are usually shortened on Saturdays, and many shops remain closed on Sundays, except in large tourist areas.

Calle Castillo – Santa Cruz
The best shopping on the island can be found in Santa Cruz. This main shopping street features recognizable brand names among local shops and independent boutiques. There are plenty of cafes, tapas, and restaurants along the street as well, so feel free to stop for refreshments as your browse.

African Market – Santa Cruz
Located on Calle San Sebastian, this colorful outdoor market is open in the early morning and afternoon throughout the week, and sells fruit, vegetables, spices, herbs, and meats. On Sunday mornings the area fills with hundreds of stalls for the weekly flea market, and it's a wonderful place to pick up bargains and souvenirs.

Centro Comercial Americas Plaza – Costa Adeje
Open from 10 am to 10 pm daily, this modern shopping mall has international retail shops as well as traditional Canarian shops. Whether you're looking for clothing or souvenirs, you'll find them here. Multiple cafés and restaurants are located in the shopping center, so you can easily spend the entire day.

Al Campo la Villa Shopping Center – La Laguna
A great selection of shops, boutiques and cafes can be found at this resort, with several other shopping centers located nearby. Again, name brand clothing can be found here, as well as Canarian goods.

Shops in Puerto de la Cruz
There isn't a single shopping district in Puerto de la Cruz, but several. The best shops can be found lining the streets near the Plaza del Charco, on the Avenido Generalisimo, on Calle de la

Hoya, and on Calle de San Felipe.

Gran Canaria

Gran Canaria is sometimes called the "miniature continent" due to its diversity – and it does justice to its nickname. And, if you just want to experience the simple pleasures of being on a beach to sunbathe and swim, Gran Canaria will meet all of your requirements. Go to Maspalomas in the south of the island, and you will find not only a beach that stretches over 8 kilometers, but also vast sand dunes. There you can spread a towel on the sand, or rent a sunbed and a parasol, and relax.

When you visit the capital city of Las Palmas, you will find the most popular beach in Gran Canaria, Playa de las Canteras. It features a golden sand beach that is 3 kilometers long and a delightful promenade to stroll upon that is just as long. A reef 200-meter long shelters the beach from the waves, and creates a natural lagoon where you will enjoy bathing.

In Gran Canaria, you can combine shopping, sightseeing, eating and drinking, when you visit El Muelle shopping center in Las Palmas. This mall, which is overlooking the Puerto de la Luz harbor, is one of the best shopping centers in Europe. It has 60 shops, a large open-air disco which is 5,000 square meters in size, and many other amenities.

If you are interested in water sports--windsurfing and kitesurfing, for example--a number of beaches and resorts in Gran Canaria are there to serve you. Those who love plants and animals will learn that the island has various species of plants, which are not seen anywhere else in the world. About half of the land area of Gran Canaria, has been declared a protected biosphere reserve by UNESCO.

Culture

The original native Canarians, called Guanches, were a mysterious group of people. They were tall and had blonde hair, features that do not match those of aborigines in other regions. They were not seafarers. They did not build boats in spite of their proximity to coastal waters.

The Guanches did not use metals and did not have the wheel. Neither did they have a written language. Their culture disappeared within a few decades of the colonization of the Canary Islands by Spain, in 1472.

But the Guanches according to legend, were noble and brave; and they are a source of much pride in the Canary Islands. In spite of their inferior weaponry, they gave a strong resistance to the invading soldiers of Spain. Many Spanish soldiers perished in the battle against the Guanches.

Folk music and dancing generally represent the present-day Canarian culture. The Pueblo Canario cultural square holds the best examples of contemporary Canarian culture. Local dancing and singing is performed on Sunday mornings at Pueblo Canario. Here you will also find the Museo Nestor, an art gallery dedicated to the life and works of symbolist and most famous painter of the island, Nestor Fernandez de la Torre.

Gran Canaria holds "fiestas" (religious festivals) which are dedicated to its many patron saints. These events, which are characterized by merrymaking in town squares in the island, are held almost throughout the year. The "fiestas" celebrate the feast day of the patron saints of villages in the island. A statue of Jesus and the Virgin Mary are paraded throughout the village, to commemorate the day. After the parade, the villagers dance and drink (mostly rum and red wine) in the town squares.

The religion of about 90% of the inhabitants of Gran Canaria is Catholic. This is because of the influence of Spain, which colonized the Canary Islands in the 15th century.

Many who arrived as immigrants in Gran Canaria, still maintain their links to their families in Cuba and Venezuela. Spanish, which is spoken in the Canary Islands, is more akin to Spanish spoken in Cuba than in mainland Spain.

Location & Orientation

Gran Canaria is one of the Canary Islands, Spain. It is located 62 kilometers east of Tenerife, and 83 kilometers west of Fuerteventura. Its east coast is flat and is dotted with beaches, while the west coast is rocky and mountainous.

Gran Canaria is located in the Atlantic Ocean, and it has the same latitude as Florida, USA. It is situated about 150 kilometers northwest of the coast of Africa, and 1,250 kilometers from Cadiz,

Spain.

Its capital is Las Palmas, which has a population of about 400,000. Gran Canaria itself has a population of close to 1,000,000. It is almost circular in shape, with a diameter of about 45 kilometers. It has a surface area of 1,553 square kilometers.

Gran Canaria and the other islands in Canary Islands, are part of Macaronesia, a group of Eastern Atlantic islands that includes the Azores, Madeira, and the Cape Verdes.

Almost 2.2 million tourists visit Gran Canaria annually. The majority of tourists stay in resorts along the southeast coast (e.g. Maspalomas and Playa del Ingles) because of the climate, beaches, and other amenities.

Climate & When to Visit

The climate in Gran Canaria is reputed to be the best in the whole of Europe, according to a study made by Syracuse University, USA. Gran Canaria gets its heat from the Sahara Desert, and it is cooled by cold waters from Northern Europe.

Gran Canaria receives an average of 8 hours of sunshine every day. Its temperature at sea level is rarely below 20°C. Because of its climate, sunshine and warmth even during winter is almost guaranteed.

Most tourists visit the southern part of the island. The northern part tends to be cooler, while the south is warm and sunny, and with less rain than the north.

The temperature in Gran Canaria is 17°C in winter, and 25°C in

Gran Canaria

summer, which is ideal for winter breaks and summer holidays. Gran Canaria and the rest of the Canarian archipelago, is a suitable destination for any time of the year.

Cheap flights are available from carriers like Jet2, RyanAir and EasyJet, year-round.

Gran Canaria Sightseeing Highlights

Las Palmas

Las Palmas is the capital of Gran Canaria. It is situated at the northeastern section of the island. With a population of about 400,000, it is the biggest city in Gran Canaria. It is situated 20 kilometers away from the Las Palmas International Airport.

Two of the most significant sites in Las Palmas are its beautiful sandy beaches, La Playa de las Canteras and Playa de las Alcaravaneras. Playa de las Alcaravaneras is near the city and is beside the Muelle Deportivo marina. This beach has one kilometer

Gran Canaria Sightseeing Highlights

of golden sand, and it is well-suited for aquatic sports, such as sailing.

Near the Playa de las Alcaravaneras is Parque Doramas. There, you will find gardens, which are home to species of "autochthonous" plants (local native plants). You will also find in this park, three significant structures: Pueblo Canario Museum, which is a sample of traditional Canarian architecture; Museo Nestor, which is a museum dedicated to Nestor Martin Fernandez de la Torre, who was a painter and a symbolist, and one of two famous brothers in Gran Canaria; and the historic Hotel Santa Catalina, which was built in colonial style, in 1890.

Pueblo Canario Museum is a complex featuring island houses built along traditional lines, and laid out to form a typical Canarian village. The design of the museum was the brainchild of Nestor Martin Fernandez de la Torre. Its contruction was done by his architect brother Miguel. Nestor was a local artist revered by the inhabitants of Gran Canaria.

Pueblo Canario is considered to be a masterpiece of both brothers and they are a source of pride to the brothers and the local inhabitants. Its large open-air central square serves as the stage for performances showing local folklore of Gran Canaria.

Puerto de la Luz, which is located near Playa de las Alcaravaneras, is considered one of the most important ports in Europe. From this site, you can watch the popular sport vela latina (Canarian lateen sailing) regattas leave for the sea almost every weekend.

A popular event held in Las Palmas during the first quarter of the year is its carnival. (See the separate section on the carnival in Las Palmas.)

Las Palmas also holds another famous festival, the Fundacionales de San Juan (Saint John Festival) to commemorate the founding of the city. It is also the feast day of St. John the Baptist, which is celebrated in other Catholic countries.

A city as large and as popular among tourists as Las Palmas, offers you its beaches, famous cultural sites, and religious festivities. But there is much more. It prides itself of having four large shopping centers: Las Arenas, which is the biggest in the island; La Ballena; 7 Palmas; and El Muelle, which is probably the best shopping center in Europe.

You can also shop for traditional products or produce of the island in four markets: Vegueta, el Puerto, Alcaravaneras, and Alta Vista. You can find craftwork on Sundays in Pueblo Canario or Vegueta. The FEDAC shop in Triana is the official outlet for craftwork. And an antique market is held on the first Sunday of each month at Santa Catalina Park. (See the separate sections on Vegueta and Triana.)

Gran Canaria Sightseeing Highlights

Las Palmas Cathedral

Playa de las Canteras, Las Palmas

Playa de las Canteras Beach is one of four beaches in Gran Canaria, and it is the most popular. A promenade Paseo de Canteras runs parallel to the beach. The presence of street entertainers, artists, and street vendors there, serves as an added attraction in the area.

Playa de las Canteras was the first tourist resort of Gran Canaria, and is bordered on the east by Santa Catalina and on the north by

Canary Islands Travel Guide

La Isleta.

The beach has a natural barrier reef known as "La Barra", which breaks the waves as they come into the beach. The reef is about 200 meters long, and is responsible for creating a natural lagoon, where you can go bathing. The beach is ideal for a number of water sports--it is considered a great spot for surfing.

In Playa de las Canteras, you can also find the biggest shopping center in Gran Canaria. It is known as Las Arenas, which is situated in front of Alfredo Kraus Auditorium at the northwest corner of the beach. (Alfredo Kraus was a famous tenor singer from Gran Canaria.)

Playa de las Canteras (Beach from the Promenade)

Gran Canaria Sightseeing Highlights

Vegueta, Las Palmas

The name "Vegueta" comes from the Spanish word "vega" which refers to a fertile plain. It is the oldest town of Las Palmas. Because of its historical and cultural significance, Vegueta has been declared a World Heritage site by UNESCO.

At Plaza Santa Ana in Vegueta, you will notice bronze statues of dogs. They symbolize the appearance of dogs in Las Palmas in the early 16th century. Gran Canaria is known as "The Island of Dogs".

The most important historical buildings in Las Palmas can be found in Vegueta. These buildings have stood for more than 500 years, namely: Chapel of San Antonio Abad, Plaza Santa Ana, Obispado, and Casa Regental. It is said that the chapel is where Christopher Columbus prayed on his first stop, on his way back from the Americas.

When you visit the Santa Ana Cathedral at Plaza Santa Ana, you will be amazed at how it had kept its original state after so many centuries. The Casa Colon or Christopher Columbus museum records the voyages to America of this famous explorer. He was known to have made a stopover in Las Palmas, and he stayed in Casa Colon before he continued his journey.

You will also find in Vegueta, the Museo Canario, which contains relics of the Guanches, the native inhabitants of the island. Another museum, The Museum of Sacred Art, displays several religious works. The town also has an old market that dates back to the 19th century.

Canary Islands Travel Guide

Vegueta Market, Las Palmas

Triana, Las Palmas

Triana is near Vegueta, and is located on one side of Guiniguada ravine. Here, you can enjoy a pleasant walk along Calle Mayor de Triana, where there are buildings of great artistic and historical value.

At San Telmo Park in Triana, you will find the chapel of San Telmo, a modern pavilion and bandstand. The park features mature landscaping with large palm trees; and this is where visitors can go during the day to experience peace in the city. You will also find there, Teatro Perez Galdos, which is a theater of Italian design and is one of the most emblematic buildings of Las Palmas.

Other architectural structures in the area surrounding Triana, are Edificio Quegles which was built in 1900; Casa Museo Perez Galdos, which contains an archive of Benito Perez Galdos, who was born in this house. He was a famous Spanish author who lived between 1843 and 1920. Aside from the sentimental value of this house, it also represents an example of 18th century Canarian architecture.

Maspalomas

From Maspalomas to its twin resort Playa del Ingles, the beach and sand dunes stretch over a distance of 8 kilometers. The sand dunes cover a vast area of 250 hectares, situated right next to the sea. Go to this area before sunset to take some great photos.

In front of the sand dunes are beautiful beaches that stretch from the famous lighthouse "El Faro" to the farthest end of Playa del Ingles. It is safe to swim in the sea in parts, but you are advised to stay close to the lifeguard towers, situated at either end of the beach.

Maspalomas Beach has an oasis-like appearance with its palm trees and sand dunes. There, you can spread your towel on the sand and have a quiet and pleasurable sunbathing experience. Sunbeds and parasols are available for rent at the beach, if you need them.

As you walk along the beach, you can always avail of café kiosks, which can be found every few hundred meters along the beach. There, you can find a cold drink, hot coffee, or some snacks.

Canary Islands Travel Guide

Visit the many 4 & 5-Star Hotels in Maspalomas - and experience the high-quality (free) evening entertainment.

Aqualand, Maspalomas

Aqualand is located near Maspalomas in the southern part of Gran Canaria on the road to Palmitos Park. Because of the favorable weather in the island, the park is open all year round.

It is the biggest water park in Gran Canaria, with a total area of 90,000 square meters. The park's pools alone have an area of 5,300 square meters. It is ideal for an outing with your family. It has 33 slides and 13 other attractions, which include Tornado, Surf

Beach, Congo River, Crazy Race, Kamikaze, Rapids, Aquamania, Twister, and many others. Tornado is the main attraction of the park, featuring an incredible slide.

You and your family can also avail of their self-service restaurants, pizzeria, coffee shops, bars, and other facilities.

You can reach Aqualand by bus. You can board either from Playa del Ingles or Bahia Feliz, or from Puerto Rico or Faro Maspalomas.

Playa del Ingles

Playa del Ingles literally means, "Beach of the English." It is considered to be the biggest and liveliest resort in Gran Canaria. It lies between the two smaller resorts, Maspalomas and San Agustin. Together they share a beach 8 kilometers long and 3 kilometers wide. From the airport it can be reached in 30 minutes by car or bus via the main highway.

Playa del Ingles is a popular beach for the young, age 18-30, particularly during the summer holidays of July and August. The rest of the year it is usually a beach which attracts tourists of all ages.

You will not find historical monuments or cultural sights in the resort. Instead, you will find--aside from the beach, of course--high-rise hotels, shopping malls, and fast-food restaurants. Established in 1960, it is now a resort that is famous throughout Europe. Two of the biggest commercial centers in Playa del Ingles are, Yumbo Centrum at Avenida de Espana, and Kasbah at Plaza Telde.

You can spend the day at the beach sunbathing, or engaging in water sports--jet skiing, skydiving, or paragliding. You can also go to the promenade Paseo Costa Canaria, which is lined with tropical flora and luxurious villas. At night, be prepared to see the scenery change, as discos and nightclubs go into action until the small hours.

If you want to devote some time for spiritual matters during your holiday at La Playa del Ingles, you can go to a church, Templo Ecumenico de San Salvador. It gives ecumenical services in three different languages.

Carnival, Gran Canaria

The carnival in Gran Canaria is an ancient tradition, which originated in the 16th century. The word "carnival" comes from the expression, "carnem levare". Literally it means, "remove the meat" or freely translated it means, "farewell to the flesh". But what a farewell party!

It is a festival that, based on Christian tradition precedes Lent, which starts on Ash Wednesday, a day of fasting, and followed by meatless meals on certain days of the Lenten season.

Through the years the carnival has evolved to what it is today. But its features have remained basically the same: processions and floats, fireworks, bizarre and colorful masks and costumes, dancers (known as "murgas" and "comparsas"), singers, merrymakers, and loud Latin music. The carnival also holds contests to select the carnival queen, the best bands, the best dancers, the best singers, and other forms of entertainment.

The carnival is taken very seriously in Gran Canaria--it can take as long as a year, to design and make the costume of the carnival queen. A contest is held to select the queen of the carnival in the

Gran Canaria Sightseeing Highlights

weeks prior to the start of the carnival, and the finalists are presented during the start of the carnival. The highlight of the festival is the crowning of the queen of the carnival.

The carnival is one of the most anticipated festivals in Gran Canaria, and it is celebrated in almost every town staggered over a period of a few days. The best carnival experiences are celebrated in Las Palmas, Playa del Ingles, Arguineguin, Agaete, and Telde. Each of the carnivals in these places has its own distinctive features, and is always participated by a great number of people.

The revelry begins at dusk and ends at dawn. Each year the carnival starts in late February, and ends on Ash Wednesday, the start of the Lenten season, which is observed by Catholics as a period of fasting and abstinence.

When you visit Gran Canaria in time for the carnival, be sure to pack your costumes and masks. You can then join the fun, and be one of the merrymakers snaking around in a procession in practically every part of the island.

Carnival in Las Palmas, 2012

Teror

Teror is one of the oldest and most beautiful towns in Gran Canaria. When you visit your attention will be drawn to the famous Basilica of the La Senora de Pino (Virgin of the Pine); and secondly, by the distinctive architectural style of the buildings.

The Basilica is a magnificent landmark dedicated to the Virgin Mary, who, some inhabitants of Gran Canaria say, appeared on its site on September 8, 1481. The town celebrates the Feast of the Virgin of the Pine on this same date every year. The festival begins with a parade featuring the centuries-old statue of the Blessed Virgin, and ends with a late night, open-air celebration, common to parties in the island.

Plaza del Pino is a vast plaza in the center of Teror, which is surrounded by elegant homes. These homes were built in characteristic colonial style, with doors, windows, and balconies made of dark carved wood. Many of these structures date back to the 1500s, and because of their unique architectural features, the center of the town of Teror was declared a national monument.

The Sunday market in Teror offers you a wide range of goods, including some of its specialties, like the spicy sausage Chorizo de Teror, sweets made by nuns in the locality, and handicrafts of various kinds.

During your visit you can also have a taste of Teror's famous mineral water, Agua de Teror, which comes from a natural spring just outside the town.

Canary Islands Travel Guide

La Cumbre

La Cumbre (The Summit) is located at the center of Gran Canaria. It is a rugged mountainous region with charming villages. It has winding roads, which you can use for a rigorous trek up the mountains. But if you are not up to this kind of activity, you can choose to have a leisurely hike along gentler roads that lead to the miradores or viewing areas. Here, you can have a breathtaking view of the surrounding landscape.

Pico de las Nieves (Snow Peak), and Roque Nublo (Cloudy Rock/ Misty Rock), are two of the top choices where you can start your sightseeing in La Cumbre. Pico de Las Nieves rises 1,950 meters high, and it is the highest point in Gran Canaria. Roque Nublo is an 80-meter monolith, which has become the emblem of Gran Canaria.

Roque Nublo is only 1,813 meters high or lower than Pico de las Nieves; you can get to its summit by hiking for about 30 minutes. As you hike, you will also come upon some miradores or viewing areas, from where you can have a view of the entire southern part of Gran Canaria, Maspalomas, Playa del Ingles, and Puerto Mogan. When you reach the summit, you will be able to see the famous monolith and the snow-capped Mount Teide on the island of Tenerife.

At Roque Nublo, you can view three other interesting rock formations known as El Fraile or The Monk, La Rana or The Frog, and Roque Bentayga, which is a pre-hispanic place of worship with cave dwellings hewn out of vertical cliffs.

The next item in your itinerary can be a visit to highland towns, first of which is Tejeda. The town is a sight to behold especially in February or March, when the winter rains make the almond trees blossom. Then, go also to another nearby town, Artenara, the smallest of the municipalities in the highlands. It is an intriguing place, where you can stop by cave homes and cave hotels. The main attraction of Artenara is a cave church, the Santuario de la Virgen Cuevita.

Palmitos Park

Palmitos Park is located 10 kilometers north of the Beach and Sand Dunes of Maspalomas and Playa del Ingles. It has an area of 20 hectares, which has been developed as a botanical garden and aviary.

The park features thousands of palm trees, a large variety of birds, orchids, and exotic creatures. Certain birds of prey and exotic birds in the park, such as falcons, parrots, and eagles are among the favorites of visitors to the park. Other types of birds can also be seen in the park, and these include swans and ducks. The park has a total of more than 1,500 exotic birds of various species, many of which are allowed to fly freely in the park.

Another significant feature of the park is its wide range of cacti and succulents in excellent condition. The park has over 160 different cactus types and 1000 palm trees of 42 different types.

The park is situated in the countryside in the midst of mountains. The location affords visitors the chance to view beautiful landscapes as they walk around the park. A small terrace leads to an amphitheater, where some birds of prey perform in shows meant for the entertainment of visitors. Beside the amphitheater is a snack bar; a small cafeteria can be found elsewhere in the park.

Canary Islands Travel Guide

Puerto de Mogan

Puerto de Mogan marina is located at the southwest coast of Gran Canaria. It is a picturesque resort and marina, which is just a 40-minute drive by car from the airport. The resort offers water sports-related services and activities. If you like adventurous sports, you can go parasailing, jet skiing, scuba diving, or take a submarine tour. If you prefer a less strenuous activity, you can take tours to watch dolphins, or take ferry rides to nearby sites.

The resort is dubbed, "La Venecia de Canarias" or "Venice of the Canaries". This is so because of the sea water channels between the marina and the harbor, which pass under arches in the buildings, and between the port and the beach. The harbor is considered to be one of the best and most popular ports in the Canary Islands.

Residential buildings in Puerto de Mogan are built in Mediterranean style, and are not more than three storeys high. They are built along narrow alleys all planted with flowers, mostly bougainvilleas.

Sioux City, Bahia Feliz

Sioux City is a make-believe western town, located in Canon del Aguila (Canyon of the Eagle) near Bahia Feliz. It covers an area of 320,000 square meters or 32 hectares. If you are not going on a group tour, it is best that you go by car or taxi as the site is a long walk from the nearest bus stop in the vicinity.

Sioux City was built as the set for a film called, "Take a Hard Ride." You will be treated to shows (there are two daily) featuring cowboys and Indians, just as in the days in the "Wild Wild West" in the USA.

Gran Canaria Sightseeing Highlights

Sioux City features cattle stampedes, gunfights, and Indians in a tepee. It will stage for you a Bank Robbery, Saloon Fight, Town Square Hanging, Indian Rain Dance, and other typical scenes that you see in western movies.

You can dine at Sioux City's Three Stars Saloon or BBQ Station. There, you can pretend that you are in a truly Western town in the USA. Who knows you might just bump into some of your Western heroes. But don't be disappointed, if one of them is not Clint Eastwood or John Wayne!

Recommendations for the Budget Traveler to Gran Canaria

Places to Stay

The principal tourist destination in the Canary Islands is Gran Canaria. For travelers who are looking for good-value hotels, Gran Canaria offers several comfortable and affordable hotels and apartments. Here are some of the recommended places to stay.

AC Hotel Gran Canaria Marriott

Recommendations for the Budget Traveler to Gran Canaria

Las Palmas 35007 Eduardo Benot, 3-5
Las Palmas de Gran Canaria, Spain
+34-928-266-100
http://www.marriott.com/hotels/travel/lpagr-ac-hotel-gran-canaria/
From $80+

AC Hotel Gran Canaria by Marriott is located in the center of the city, about 300 meters from the famous Las Canteras Beach. You can walk to Sta. Catalina Park and the Museo Elder de la Ciencia from the hotel. The main shopping area is just a 10-minute stroll. The hotel is easily accessible from the airport, which is around 20 kilometers away. Each room is air-conditioned and is equipped with cable TV, broad band Internet access for a surcharge, free mini bar that is replenished daily, a private bathroom and a big, comfortable bed. It has a rooftop swimming pool where you can view the whole city, the ocean, and the surrounding mountains.

Club Hotel Riu Gran Canaria
Las Meloneras, 35100 Maspalomas
Gran Canaria, Spain
 +34-928-56 30 00
From $64+

Located at the seafront on Costa Meloneras, this hotel is built amidst a 30,000-square meter garden. It is around 900 meters from Maspalomas Beach and the Sand Dunes, 200 meters from various shops, and 100 meters from a bus stop. From the hotel you can explore nearby sites like Playa de los Burras, Mogan Harbor, and the historical town of Aguimes. All rooms are air-conditioned and equipped with modern facilities, such as mini fridge, satellite TV, private bathroom, and telephone. Wireless internet is available at the lobby for a surcharge. It has 3 swimming pools for adults, a swimming pool for children, and 2 whirlpools.

Cordial Mogan Valle, Puerto de Mogan
Avda los Marrero 4

Canary Islands Travel Guide

35138 Puerto de Mogan
Gran Canaria, Spain
+34 928143393
www.cordialcanarias.com/en/index.html
Rate: $72+

The hotel is situated in the middle of a 35,000-square meter garden in Puerto Mogan, which is known as the "Little Venice" of Gran Canaria. It is just a few meters away from the beach, the marina, and the fishing quay. The hotel consists of apartments with one or two bedrooms. Each apartment is furnished with a microwave oven, coffee maker, fridge, satellite TV, direct dial telephone, and a private bathroom with shower. There are three swimming pools for adults and a children's pool. Wi-Fi is available in the whole hotel area.

Hotel Terraza Amadores
Islas Afortunadas 1, Puerto Rico
Gran Canaria, Spain
Tel: +0034-928725613
Website: www.terrazadeamadores.com
Rate: $42+

The hotel is an apartment complex conveniently located in front of Playa Amadores Beach. Although it is close to the shopping area (only 300 meters from the nearest commercial center), it still retains its tranquil and peaceful atmosphere. Each apartment is clean and well maintained, and has a living room furnished with a sofa bed and a TV. It has a bathroom with private shower, and a kitchenette with a fridge, microwave oven, and coffee maker. Internet via modem is available in all public areas of the hotel for a surcharge. It offers great food and drinks at reasonable prices. The hotel's swimming pool for adults and pool for children are kept clean at all times.

Riu Palace Maspalomas

Recommendations for the Budget Traveler to Gran Canaria

Avda Tirajana S/n Playa del Engles, Maspalomas
San Bartolome de Tirajana
35100 Spain
Tel: +34928769800
Rate: $83+

The hotel is situated close to Maspalomas Beach and Sand Dunes. It is designed in colonial-style architecture very much like a huge Roman amphitheater. It is near Yumbo shopping center and other attractions, such as the Palmitos Park and Amadores Beach. The air-conditioned rooms open to balconies or terraces and are equipped with amenities, which include a private bathroom, telephone, mini-bar, and a satellite TV. It is located 30 kilometers from the airport, and 50 meters from the nearest bus stop. It has an outdoor pool, a sauna and a Jacuzzi. The hotel restaurant serves a variety of delicious food for both vegetarians and meat lovers alike.

Canary Islands Travel Guide

Places to Eat & Drink

You have plenty of restaurants to choose from in Gran Canaria, depending on your taste and budget. Here are a few of the recommended restaurants in the Island.

Mama Mia, Playa del Ingles
Centro Commercial Yumbo, Lower Floor
35100 Playa del Ingles
Gran Canaria, Spain
+34 633346899
www.mammamiagrancanaria.com

Recommendations for the Budget Traveler to Gran Canaria

Mamma Mia is an Italian restaurant in the Yumbo Center. They serve authentic, classic Italian food, complete with primo and secondi items.

La Oliva, Las Palmas
c/Prudencio Morales 17
35009 Las Palmas de Gran Canaria
Gran Canaria, Spain
+34 928469757

La Oliva is a very busy and crowded restaurant known for its delicious tapas. The seafood dishes are superb, especially their fried calamares. The service is great and the prices are very reasonable.

Amadores Beach Club Restaurant, Puerto Rico
Playa Amadores, Puerto Rico
Gran Canaria, Spain

The menu is varied with a lot of fusion type meals, from seafood to steaks, to sushi and Mexican dishes, all at reasonable prices. It is a great location to watch the sunset, while enjoying your meal.

Restaurante La Tapita-Los Jose's in Maspalomas
Placido Domingo 12, Maspalomas
Gran Canaria, Spain
+34 928769680

The restaurant serves quality tapas at a reasonable price. The house wine is good and the service is excellent. Without a doubt, the place deserves a second visit.

Fusion Restaurant & Loungebar, Arguineguin
Calle Alonzo Quesada 13, 35120 Arguineguin
Gran Canaria, Spain

+34 926185662
www.fusionrestaurantandloungebar.com

Excellent delicious food, excellent value, with a soothing and relaxing ambiance. The lunchtime special is highly recommended. The staff are extremely friendly and the restaurant is well worth a visit.

Places to Shop

Gran Canaria has a lot of shops, malls, and other establishments that cater to tourists who visit this beautiful island. With its busy port, street markets, and low duties on imported goods, Gran

Recommendations for the Budget Traveler to Gran Canaria

Canaria has become a shoppers' haven in Europe. Here are some of the places to go to if you are looking for souvenirs, presents, or other items that might catch your fancy.

El Muelle Shopping Center – Centro Commercial El Muelle
Muelle de Santa Catalina s/n
35008 Las Palmas de Gran Canaria
Gran Canaria, Spain
+34928327527

This shopping center is considered one of the best shopping centers in Europe. It is located inside the harbor near Parque Santa Catalina. It has 60 shops including clothing shops, such as Zara, Mango, Barshka, Benetton, and Massimo Dutti. There are also shoe shops selling shoes "to die for", handbag shops selling leather bags and cases, costume jewelry shops, perfume shops, sports shops, and many more. Catch the number 40 bus, get off at Parque Santa Catalina, and take the lift to the ground floor – that's the easiest way to El Muelle.

Avenida Mesa y Lopez, Las Palmas
Avenida Mesa y Lopez, is a shopping street near the famous Parque Santa Catalina in Las Palmas. The whole street is lined with beautiful trees and shops. All the major chain stores in Spain are here, including El Corte Ingles, the largest department store in the country. Marks & Spencers is also here. There are benches in the middle of the street where you can sit to take a rest, and refresh yourself, before you go on your next shopping spree.

Calle Mayor de Triana of Las Palmas
This pedestrian street is lined with good shops from stylish upmarket outlets to small shops selling local goods, and from exclusive boutiques to Indian bazaars. There are lots of retail clothing shops and plenty of shops selling shoes at attractive prices. A shoppers' haven, it is also a place where you can see examples of old Canarian architecture. There are also a lot of cafes

for the tired shoppers, who wish to rest before more shopping activities.

Pueblo Canario (Canarian Village)
Parque Doramas
Las Palmas de Gran Canaria, 35005
Gran Canaria, Spain
+34 928242985
www.pueblocanarop.es/

The main reason why the brothers Nestor and Miguel Martin Fernandez de la Torre built Pueblo Canario, was to create interest among tourists in Canarian culture. The buildings inside the village are designed in traditional Canarian architecture. Besides restaurants and a chapel, there are also handicraft shops here, where you can buy souvenirs and gifts for friends and relatives back home.

FEDAC – Playa del Ingles
cnr Avenida Espana & Avenida EE UU, Playa del Ingles
Centro Insular del Turismo
Gran Canaria, Spain
+34928772445

If you are looking for local handicrafts, FEDAC is the place for you. It is a government sponsored, non-profit shop, where you can buy souvenirs and presents for your friends and relatives back home.

Lanzarote

Lanzarote is home to some of the most unusual and startling landscapes on the planet. Because of its volcanic history, the island is covered with lava formations, and you may feel like you have stepped out of this world and onto the surface of the moon.

Between the dry climate and the lack of erosion, the landscape looks much as it did when volcanoes were active several centuries ago. The volcanic activity of the past few eons has created incredible craters and cave systems just waiting to be explored, including the longest volcanic tunnel in the world, The Atlantida Tunnel, which stretches over 7 km.

But slumbering volcanoes aren't the only things making Lanzarote worth visiting...213 km of coastline make for stunning beaches, and the views of the sparkling water will take your breath away. Regulations regarding development have made sure that Lanzarote remains quaint and picturesque, with no billboard advertising, and very few high-rise buildings.

Whether you prefer the excitement of Carnival or the quiet

relaxation of the beach, Lanzarote is bound to become a favorite vacation spot. And the small size of the island means you can enjoy it all without long drives or flights.

Culture

Having been settled since 1000 BC, the island of Lanzarote has a rich history. The Phoenicians, Arabs, and Castilians have all claimed Lanzarote as their own, and in the 17th century, it was even raided by pirates! Today, the island is claimed by Spain and the population of 139,000 is mostly Spaniard.

The culture of Lanzarote is a unique blending of ancient traditions

Lanzarote

and European ideals brought over from Spain. Place names are occasionally in the aboriginal language of the Guanches, but modern life has taken hold of day-to-day living.

Castilian Spanish is the national language, although the dialect and accent is closer to that of other Latin American countries than Spain. The population is largely Roman Catholic, and religion plays an important part in the culture of the island.

Despite the harsh conditions of Lanzarote, the people of the island have managed to cultivate the land, and fruit and vegetable plantations can be found throughout the island. But the main industry is tourism, with 80% of the island's residents involved in the industry in some way or another.

Even though millions of visitors come to the island each year, Lanzarote maintains many of its cultural traditions. Traditional folk music is played on the timple, a ukulele-like instrument that has been played in Lanzarote since the 15th century. The timple is the instrument of choice at local fiestas, accompanying dances like the isa and folia, and even the tajaraste, the only dance said to have been passed down from the aboriginal Guanches.

Lanzarote also continues the unique tradition of Lucha Canaria, a form of wrestling where contestants attempt to throw each other to the ground inside a 12-meter ring. The people of Lanzarote consider themselves more "Canarios" than Spaniards, and take pride in their strong connection with the land.

Lanzarote was also a destination for artists and writers, and the influence of these poets, novelists, and painters can be seen everywhere. Several museums pay homage to their works, but many visitors find that the island itself is one large interactive museum to the history, art, and culture of the people who have lived there.

Canary Islands Travel Guide

Orientation & Location

Located 127 km off the coast of Morroco in Africa, Lanzarote is the most easterly of the Canary Islands. It is the fourth largest of the Canary Islands, at 60 km long and 20 km wide. Even so, it is only about half the size of the U.S. state of Rhode Island. It is also the closest island to Spain, lying just 1000 km to the southwest.

The powerful volcanic eruptions that took place at Timanfaya between 1730 and 1736 have influenced much of the landscape, although far more ancient eruptions have also left their mark. The Timanfaya eruptions of the 1700s marks the most powerful and longest lasting period of volcanic activity in recorded history.

Today, Timanfaya is a 51 sq km National Park entirely made up of volcanic soil. Though Lanzarote is small, the island has two mountain ranges: the 671 km Famara in the north, and the 608 km Ajaches in the south. The El Jable desert lies just south of the Famara.

There are over 500 varieties of plants and lichen on the island, and the harsh volcanic environment has caused many plants to adapt to life with a scarcity of water. Thirty-five types of animals live on the island, including one of two surviving populations of the endangered Canarian Egyptian Vulture.

Climate & When to Visit

At 29°00' north, 13°40' west, Lanzarote enjoys a mild, dry climate year-round, making it an ideal destination no matter when you're

Lanzarote

traveling.

However, the island has two high seasons: from November to April and from July to August. If you'd prefer to avoid the crowds and enjoy off-season deals on hotels and flights, May to June or September to October are ideal times to travel.

You may also wish to plan your visit around one of Lanzarote's many festivals. If you'd like to catch Lanzarote's unique Carnival, plan to visit the island between February and March. Dia de Canarias celebrates the day the Canary Islands were granted autonomy from Spain, and takes place on May 30th each year.

Fiesta de Nuestra Senora de Los Dolores is a unique festival that takes place in August or September. Locals in traditional dress make a pilgrimage to Mancha Blanca, the sight of the last volcanic eruption in 1824.

Dia Del Reyes takes place from January 5-6. Three Kings ride on camels throughout the island, giving sweets to local children. Most of the festivities surrounding Dia Del Reyes are centered in Arrecife and Puerto del Carmen.

But if you aren't interested in festivals, the autumn months from September to October are the best time to visit Lanzarote. Temperatures are just right and the North Easterly Trade Winds that blow through the island from March to August have died down. The waters of various beaches also tend to be warmer during these months.

Canary Islands Travel Guide

Lanzarote Sightseeing Highlights

Arrecife

Make plans to visit the capital city of Arrecife. Shopping, culture, and historical landmarks make this sophisticated metropolis a must for any traveler to Lanzarote.

Located right in the middle of Lanzarote's east coast, Arrecife began as a small fishing village in the 15th century, growing until it became the island's capital in 1852. Today, it is home to around 50,000 people--nearly half of the island's population.

Canary Islands Travel Guide

Centro Insular de Cultura El Almacen is one of the main attractions in Arrecife. Housed in a renovated warehouse, the cultural center consists of various exhibitions, a cinema showing original-version films, and a bar/restaurant named after Picasso, where visitors can enjoy live music on the weekends. The Centro is open from 8 am to 3 pm, Monday through Friday. For more info, call 34 928 81 01 21.

Arrecife also has two beaches: Playa de Reducto and Playa del Cable. With warm, tranquil waters and golden sand, both are excellent places for swimming and relaxation. A 2 km promenade runs between the two beaches, if you'd like to experience both in the same day and enjoy a little walk in the sun.

Various plazas and parks are located throughout the city, perfect for picnicking or reading. If you'd like to take a break from the great outdoors, Arrecife also has several cinemas, malls and restaurants. The nightlife of Lanzarote is centered in Arrecife, and an exciting selection of bars and nightclubs will keep you dancing until the wee small hours of the morning.

Accommodations are plentiful in the city, with options for every budget. Some hotels and resorts offer packages with discounts on various activities in the city. Be sure to check with your accommodations for information.

Lanzarote Sightseeing Highlights

Arrecife's Beautiful City Beach

Timanfaya National Park

Located on the western coast north of Yaiza, Timanfaya National Park is the site of the famous 1700s volcanic eruptions. Its 51 sq km is entirely made up of volcanic soil. Access to the park is strictly regulated in order to protect the unique flora and fauna of the area.

Known for its unique martian landscape, Timanfaya is a breathtaking glimpse at nature's power. You can take a coach trip around the National Park, the cost of which is included in the entry fee. You can also reserve a free guided walk by calling 48 hours in advance, or pay a little extra to take a camel ride across the volcanic landscape.

Upon entrance to the park, visitors are given a thrilling demonstration of just how hot the area is. Temperatures reach between 400 and 600 degrees Celsius just a few meters beneath the surface. Water poured onto the ground evaporates immediately, and water poured into a hole in the ground erupts seconds later in the form of a mini-geyser of steam. Dry brush thrown into that same hole catches fire immediately.

While you're there, be sure to visit "El Diablo Restaurant," which uses geothermal heat to cook its fare. There are few restaurants in the world that use a cast-iron grill placed over a large hole in the ground, so don't miss the opportunity to eat food cooked by a volcano! Visitors should know that the kitchen closes at 3 pm, so make sure to stop there early in the day.

Admission to the park is 8 euros, which includes the coach tour fee. The park is open daily from 10 am to 6 pm. For more information, call 34 928 84 00 57.

Carnival

Many people don't know that the island of Lanzarote has its very own Carnival, but the celebrations in the Canary Islands are some of the biggest outside of Rio de Janeiro in Brazil. The week-long celebration includes parades, costumes, music, dancing, and food, and is a spectacle not to be missed.

Carnival is a public celebration that takes place just before the Christian Lent, and it gives everyone an opportunity to let their hair down a little. Because Lent falls at slightly different times each calendar year, Carnival can take place anywhere from January to March. You can check online to find out when Carnival will happen during the year you're traveling.

In Lanzarote, Carnival festivities begin in Arrecife, then move through Puerto Del Carmen and Playa Blanca, before ending in Costa Teguise. You can either follow the Carnival from city to city, or just enjoy the party on the nights you're there. Parades and concerts are the main entertainments, with plenty of opportunities to join in the dancing.

"Murgas" are a popular part of Carnival. These theatrical and musical performers take advantage of the party to poke fun at politics and current events. A murga is usually performed by 15 to 17 men, and usually lasts about 45 minutes, and is a fun part of the "anything goes" atmosphere of Carnival.

A Carnival Queen is elected in a grand gala ceremony at the beginning of the festival, and much of the spectacle centers on her. Carnival in Lanzarote also selects a Carnival Drag Queen. Both Queens get places of honor in the Carnival parade.

For those traveling with children, Carnival may not be the best time to visit Lanzarote, although there are children's activities in the early evening in most cities. But there are no guarantees of quiet at any hour of the day or night, and certain streets and businesses may be closed for the festivities.

The party usually really gets going at around midnight and lasts until 6 or 8 am, so you may want to indulge in the local tradition of an afternoon siesta during Carnival! Many local businesses are closed during Carnival because of the festivities, so shopping and excursion plans may need to be adjusted if you're traveling during Carnival.

Carnival has a theme each year, so if you're planning on joining in the festivities, you can even plan a costume based on the theme. Carnival dates, themes, and other details can be found at http://www.lanzarote.com/carnival/.

Cueva de los Verdes

Lanzarote's volcanic history has created a startling system of caves within the Monumento Natural del Malpaís de La Corona. The caves are roughly 3,000 years old, and are the result of eruptions from the nearby Monte Corona.

The caves were formed when lava flows cooled on top, hardening into a solid crust as the liquid lava below continued to flow out to sea, leaving a tunnel behind. In some places, the tunnel roofs collapsed, creating individual caves.

One of these tunnels, the "Tunnel of Atlantis" is the longest submerged volcanic tunnel in the world, stretching to 7 km. The

Lanzarote Sightseeing Highlights

caves also vary in altitude, stretching from 6 km above sea level to 1.5 km below sea level.

The caves were privately owned until 1964, when a 2 km long pathway was opened to visitors. Today, guided tours are available through these caves and the famed "Tunnel of Atlantis." Sophisticated lighting allows visitors to truly appreciate the beauty of these natural wonders.

The name "Cueva de los Verdes" means the "Green Caves," but contrary to their name, the caves aren't green. Their name came from their previous owners, the Green family. The caves are also famous for the 500-seat concert hall that's been created at the entrance to the caves.

If you are visiting in October, be sure to visit the caves for the Visual Music Festival. Organized in 1989, this civic event combines contemporary music with the island's natural wonders. Concerts take place in Cueva de los Verdes, as well as in Jameos del Agua, Volcan del Cuervo, and the Santo Domingo Convent.

The caves have a rich cultural history in addition to their fascinating geological history. Back when pirates and slave traders raided the islands, the people of Lanzarote hid in the caves to prevent capture.

Be sure to stop by Jameos del Agua while you're in the area. Tours through these caves are separate from Cueva de los Verdes, but it's well worth the trip to see the stunning underground lake. You may even catch a glimpse of the famed blind white crab, a creature unique to Lanzarote.

Located in the city of Haria on the northeast corner of the island, the caves are open daily from 10 am to 6 pm, with the last trip at 5 pm. The best times to visit the caves are from 3 pm to 5 pm. Cost is 8 euros per person. For more information, call 34 928.17.32.20.

Wine Museum of Lanzarote

In operation since 1775, the El Grifo wineries are the oldest in the Canary Islands. The buildings making up the winery were built over the lava left from the eruptions of the 1730s. Each building is made of volcanic stone and mortar, with ceiling beams made from the wood salvaged from shipwrecks.

Several-hundred-year-old tools and machinery from the winery have been preserved and are on display at the museum. Because of Lanzarote's remoteness, many of these tools were used for several decades after new tools were developed elsewhere in the world.

Today, vertical hydraulic presses and stainless steal vinification equipment have replaced the equipment that is now on display at the museum. But the Moscatel vines that produce wine-grapes have been maintained since 1881, and the palm tree that presides over the estate is one of the tallest and oldest on the island, having stood since 1750.

Today, all of the work of the vineyard is done manually. Everything from the grape farming to the bottling is done on the property. The vineyard produces 400,000 to 600,000 bottles per year, and has won numerous awards.

The 61.5-hectare vineyard is owned and maintained by brothers Juan Jose Rodriguez and Fermin Otamendi Bethencourt, fifth generation of the two families that have owned the vineyard since 1880. Many of the customers who buy from the vineyard have been doing so for generations.

Lanzarote Sightseeing Highlights

The volcanic soil is excellent for farming, but to lack of rainfall throughout the year and constant trade winds make it difficult to grow grapes. The workers of the vineyard have addressed these challenges by building protective walls of volcanic rock and spreading layers of lava gravel over the soil to prevent evaporation of water.

Guided tours are available of the wine cellar Mondays through Fridays at 10:30 am, and of the museum and vineyards Mondays through Fridays at 11 am. The vineyard also has a library of over 5,000 books on the subject of wine.

The museum is open to the public every day of the year from 10:30 am to 6 pm. The entrance fee is 3 euros for adults, and includes a free wine tasting. For more information, call 34 928 52 49 51, or visit http://www.elgrifo.com/en.

Beaches

A must for all Lanzarote travelers! Surfing, snorkeling, diving, and swimming are usually available at various beaches. Check with your hotel to see what's offered nearby.

Located at the southern tip of the island, the Papagayo Beaches in Playa Blanca are some of the best on the island. Between the crystal clear waters and fine golden sand, you'll think you've stepped right into paradise. Be sure to bring your own towels and umbrellas, since there aren't any facilities that offer them. There is a café at the top of one of the beaches, but most visitors bring their own snacks and drinks.

You can drive to the beach through the Monumento Natural de Los Ajaches National Park. Entry to the park is 3 euros per car. You can also take the Princesa Yaiza Papagayo Boat from the Playa Blanca harbor for 15 euros. If you're willing to spend the extra cash, the boat is a great way to see the wildlife through the boat's glass bottom. It returns throughout the day to pick up those wishing to return to Playa Blanca.

Also at the southern tip of the island, Playa Dorada is a short walk from Playa Blanca's town center. The water is clear, calm and shallow, making it an ideal beach for swimming, especially for children. Sunbeds and umbrellas are available to rent, and several restaurants and bars are within walking distance.

Playa Famara in northwest Lanzarote is another highly recommended beach. Its stunning waves make it ideal for surfers. However, the weather can be a bit windy and the water has strong currents, so it may not be ideal for swimming or sunbathing.

In the northeast of Lanzarote, La Garita Beach in Arrieta is another beach. Arrieta is a quaint traditional fishing village off the beaten path, and is another great beach for surfing. You can access the beach from the LZ-1 coastal road, and there are several restaurants nearby.

Farther inland in Yaiza, El Golfo is a green lagoon formed from past volcanic activity. Black sands contrast with the green water, which gets its color from algae. The stunning landscape has been used in several films, and is sure to enchant you as well.

Museum of International and Contemporary Art

Housed in the 18th century Castillo de San Jose in the capital city of Arrecife, the collection is a unique and fascinating collection of culture and art. It's a modest but impressive exhibit, focusing on painting and sculpture.

The building itself is a part of the exhibit. The historic fortress was originally constructed in 1774, as a center for the alleviation of hunger and poverty caused by the volcanic eruptions of the 1730s.

As a result, it quickly became known as The Fortress of Hunger. In the years that followed, Spanish soldiers at the Castillo worked together to drive the British away.

Today, the museum's creation can be attributed to Lanzarote's own artist/architect Cesar Manrique. In the early 1970s, he persuaded the government to allow him to restore the Castillo building, and in 1976, the museum opened its doors to the public.

The museum houses works by international artists, including Alechins, Bacon, Botero, Dámaso, Domínguez, Fráncis, Leparc, Millares, Miró, Picasso, Rompó, Tápies, Luis Féito, and the founder Manrique himself. It also regularly hosts temporary exhibits and conferences.

The attached museum restaurant is also one of the best on the island, featuring international and local cuisine. The elegant seating includes views to Naos port and the docks of Mármoles, and visitors won't be disappointed by the edible works of art on their plates.

The museum is open daily from 11 am to 8 pm. Admission is 2.50 euros for adults and 1.25 euros for children. The restaurant is open daily from 1 pm to 4 pm and from 7 pm to 11:30 pm. For more information, call 34 928 80 79 29.

Jardin de Cactus

Cactus plants thrive in the dry climate of Lanzarote, and in the northern area of Guatiza, over 10,000 types of plants live as proof. Developed under the guidance of island artist/architect Cesar Manrique, the cactus garden is one of the most popular attractions year-round.

Lanzarote Sightseeing Highlights

The entire garden is a celebration of the world's spiniest plant, and each plant is displayed to their optimum effect against the backdrop of a stunning amphitheatre hewn from an old quarry. The cactus theme is repeated in more than just the plants...door handles, wrought iron gates, and sculptures throughout the garden also sport cactus shapes.

Eminent botanist Estanislao Gonzales Ferrer headed up the plant selection, design, and layout of the garden. The impressive collection of cacti and other succulents hail from the Canary Islands, America, and Madagascar.

The cactus garden also gives visitors an opportunity to learn more about what was once the mainstay of a thriving Lanzarote industry. The Tuneri cactus attracts conchineal beetles. Their crushed larvae, once scraped from the plant, were once used to create a natural dye. Today, artificial dyes have replaced the cochineal beetle colorants, but since it's not toxic, it's still used in certain food and drink items.

The Tuneri cactus is just one of the thousands of species of cactus on display, and you'll be astounded at the incredible complexities and colors of cacti you encounter. Certain times of year, various cactus plants sprout stunning flowers. After you've explored the garden, stop for refreshments at the stylish bar, located at the rear of the garden, beneath the restored Gofio mill.

The cactus garden is open daily from 10 am to 5:45 pm, and entrance fees are 5 euros for adults, and 2.50 euros for children. If you get lost on your way to the garden, look up...an 8 m high green metallic cactus statue stands guard at the main entrance.

Surf School

Canary Islands Travel Guide

Established in 2001, Lava Flow Surf School in Puerto Del Carmen is one of the best-known surf schools in the world. It focuses on giving everyone the opportunity to experience the thrill of surfing while teaching the importance of water safety. Anyone who's ever dreamed of learning to surf will find their dreams coming true here.

The director and senior surf instructor has been surfing for over 20 years, 13 of which he has spent on the island of Lanzarote. His qualifications include Royal Lifesaving Beach Lifeguard, pool lifeguard, and International Lifesaving Society Surf Lifeguard. He is also the only non-Spanish person to hold the F.E.S.S. award.

Located in Puerto del Carmen, the school does a daily assessment to decide which waves will best meet their clients surfing ability. They provide a safe and fun learning environment for surfing students of all ages and experience levels. The staff hold up-to-date first aid and life-saving certificates.

Classes are open to people of all ages and experience levels. The school also has a 100% success rate, with clients ranging from ages 8 to 63, and guarantee that each student will stand up surfing after finishing their course with the school.

A 1-day surf course includes transfer from hotel/apartment to and from Famara Beach (pick up time 9 am – 9:30 am and return time 3 pm), surfboards and wet suits, surf lesson theory and practical, lunch on Famara Beach, one-on-one coaching, and a photograph. Cost is 40 euros per adult and 25 euros per child under 11.

If you're looking for more extensive lessons, the school also offers a 3-day course that includes all of the same thing as the 1-day course, as well as a Lavaflow Surf Lanzarote Merit Diploma. Cost is 110 euros for adults and 75 euros for children under 11.

Lanzarote Sightseeing Highlights

And, if you're truly serious about surfing, the school offers a variety of week-long camps. Accommodations are provided, in Eco Yurts, private apartments, or luxury villas, and costs run from 295 euros to 450 euros, depending on your package.

Lavaflow Surf School also offers courses in Stand Up Paddle Surfing, a fun sport that allows you to connect with the water, discover new ecosystems, stay fit, and relax. Stand Up Paddle Surfing consists of standing on a special surfboard and using a long paddle to propel yourself forward. Stand Up Paddle Surfing is not only recreational...it's also a form of transportation, and indigenous peoples throughout the world have traveled from island to island in this unique way.

Lavaflow Surf School also sells quality surfboards and wet suits, as well as other equipment. Their knowledgeable staff is available to help you make a selection if you'd like to invest in your own board and suit.

For more information, call 34 636 39 15 49, or visit http://www.lavaflowsurf.com/.

Lively Lady Show Bar

Considered suitable for all ages, this restaurant in Costa Teguise is a comedy drag show bar consisting of comedy mime, live singing, and audience participation. Ranked number one of all the attractions in Costa Teguise, your visit to Lanzarote won't be complete without a trip to this cabaret.

Families are welcome to the shows, and the Lively Ladies bill themselves as "good, clean family entertainment." Karaoke sing-alongs take place after every show. You can even have a recording of your karaoke put on a CD as a souvenir!

Canary Islands Travel Guide

If visitors are apprehensive, they need only read the reviews to convince them to take the chance and check out this show. The witty banter will have you laughing all night, and the music warrants standing ovations. The staff is friendly and welcoming, the atmosphere clean, and the entertainment top notch.

In fact, the shows are so good that many visitors return on a regular basis. Most visitors leave on first-name basis with the stars and owners. Costa Teguise is on the quiet side in the evenings, so if you're looking for a good night's entertainment, you can visit the bar every night you're in town. Since they do a different show each night, you won't see the same thing twice.

Shows start between 8 pm and 10 pm nightly and there's no entrance fee, although visitors are encouraged to grab a bite to eat or something to drink while watching the show. The drinks are also cheaper here than at most other bars on the island. Visitors should not that there are no shows on Thursday nights, although the bar is still open for your enjoyment. The Lively Ladies Show Bar is located in CC Calipso on Avenida de las Islas Canaries.

Lanzarote Sightseeing Highlights

Recommendations for the Budget Traveler to Lanzarote

Places to Stay

The island of Lanzarote is fairly small, so even if you plan excursions throughout the island, you can stay in one hotel for your entire trip if you wish. If you'd like to spend several days in an area before moving on, affordable accommodations can be found at various hotels and resorts throughout the island.

Santa Rosa in Costa Teguise
Avda del Mar 19, 35509 Costa Teguise
34 928 09 02 42
http://www.lanzarote-tour.com/lanzarote/apartments/

Recommendations for the Budget Traveler to Lanzarote

apartamentos_santa_rosa/santa_rosa.php
from $38 - $74/night
A Traveler's Choice 2012 winner, this hotel is a great place to stay whether you're on a romantic getaway or traveling with family. The hotel has a fitness center and restaurant, a swimming pool, and rooms come with kitchenettes. Free breakfast is offered in the mornings. The hotel is only a 10 minute walk from the nearest beach, and various restaurants and shops are situated nearby.

Nautilus Bungalows in Puerto del Carmen
Calle Gramillo 5, 35510 Puerto Del Carmen
34 928 51 44 00
http://www.nautilus-lanzarote.com/lang/index.php
from $74/night
This quiet hotel is ideal for travelers of any age, and it includes room service and a restaurant, shuttle bus service, a swimming pool, and a bar/lounge. This is an excellent choice for those with disabilities...the owners and staff have made an effort to make the entire hotel wheel-chair accessible, with uniquely-adapted bungalows for guests with special needs. They even have a special "casa del artista"...a bungalow specially adapted to the needs of artists wishing to capture the views!

Lancelot Hotel in Arrecife
Avenida Mancomunidad 9, 35500 Arrecife
34 928 59 30 03
http://www.lanzarote.com/reservas/hotellancelot
from $59/night
A simple hotel targeted to the general traveler, this hotel's friendly and helpful staff and clean rooms will make you feel right at home! The hotel is situated right on the beach, and visitors can pay a little extra for a room with an ocean view. Hotel amenities include a swimming pool, gym and restaurant. The rooms are larger than average, and the breakfast buffet receives rave reviews.

Hotel Diamar in Arrecife

Avda. Fred Olsen 8, 35500 Arrecife
34 928 81 56 65
http://www.hoteldiamar.es/presentaing.htm
from $61/night
Another charming hotel with an ocean view, amenities at this hotel include free high-speed internet, a restaurant and room service, and car rentals. Reducto beach is only a few steps away, and the city of Arrecife a few steps in the opposite direction. A little extra money will buy you a room with an ocean view, and you can watch the waves from your balcony as the sun sets.

Jardines del Sol
35570 Playa Blanca
http://jardinesdelsollanzarote.com/
from $59/night
The friendly and helpful staff at Jardines del Sol aren't the only thing to recommend this hotel...fully fitted kitchens and flat-screen TVs with English-speaking channels in every room make it a home away from home. Many bungalows include 2 bathrooms; ideal if you're traveling with family. The hotel is also wheelchair accessible, making it ideal for those with disabilities. And feel free to play a game of chess on the giant chessboard located next to the pool!

Places to Eat & Drink

Restaurants and fast food places with familiar names like "KFC" and "McDonalds" can be found throughout the island.

Restaurante El Navarro in Costa Teguise
Avenida del Mar, 13, Costa Teguise
34 928 59 21 45
Don't let looks deceive you...the average décor fades into the back of your mind as you sample some of the best food on the island.

Recommendations for the Budget Traveler to Lanzarote

Feel free to walk in, but reservations are best, since the restaurant fills quickly on a nightly basis. This is the perfect place for a special dinner or late-night drink. Be prepared to pay a little more than average prices, but this is a restaurant that even travelers on a budget can afford to splurge on!

TJ's Caribbean Tapas Bar in Puerto del Carmen
8 Calle Teide, Old Town, 35510 Puerto del Carmen
34 689 81 58 06
This Caribbean restaurant is perfect for family meals or late-night drinks. The jerk chicken is famous, as well as the rum punch, and the owners Tony and Jeanette make visitors feel welcome. Expect good portions and fast service. Walk ins are welcome, but reservations can also be made, and if you're there during the busy season, it may be a good idea to call ahead.

Poppadom Indian Restaurant in Arrecife
Centro Comercial Maritimo, Local 9D, Avenida de Las Playas, 35510 Arrecife
34 928 51 52 82
$13 - $36
The bustling city of Arrecife has dozens of highly recommended restaurants, but this multi-award winning Indian food chain is sure to hit the spot. It opened its doors in Arrecife in July of 2011, and has received rave reviews ever since. The extensive menu gives you a wide variety of choices, but if you'd like something you don't see, feel free to ask if it's available...the kitchen is very accommodating!

Atlantico Bar Restaurant in Playa Blanca
Av. Papagayo no. 75 local 13, 35580 Playa Blanca
34 656 97 30 60
https://www.facebook.com/AtlanticoRestaurant?sk=wall
$9 - $23
The seafood is best at this family-owned restaurant, and outdoor seating provides a view of the ocean. Things are quieter in the early

evening--around 7 or 8 pm--if you're looking for a relaxed meal, but it's also open until 1 am most nights if you're looking for a great late night eatery. Feel free to ask a local if you're having trouble finding it...the restaurant is located on the road behind the main group of restaurants on the sea front, opposite a church and above Rental Car.

La Ermita Tapas Bar in Tias
Av. Central 57, 35572 Tias
34 928 52 40 76
$9 - $23
This popular restaurant recommends that you get there early, or make reservations--they're usually full by 8 or 9 pm! Vegetarian options and a rich wine selection make the menu stand out from the rest, and visitors love the atmosphere.

Places to Shop

The small island of Lanzarote has many shopping opportunities. Commercial centers full of retail stores, designer label shops, independent boutiques, and outdoor markets all make for a shopper's paradise!

Always be sure to carry cash, as some local vendors may not accept cards or traveler's checks. But if you forget, there are plenty of ATMs and banks in every major city. Haggling is expected in local shops and at outdoor markets.

The Canary Islands enjoy a special Duty Free tax status, and cigarettes, alcohol, perfumes, and petrol are much cheaper in the islands than in the rest of the European Union. However, there are strict limits on how much you can bring into other EU countries. Be sure to check on item limits before attempting to travel back to the

Recommendations for the Budget Traveler to Lanzarote

mainland with your goods.

There are also many electrical goods shops that sell cameras, video cameras, and other travel electronics. But be sure to ask a local or your hotel for a recommendation...not all of these shops are reputable! Also note that the tag price is always negotiable for these goods as well as others.

Calle Real in Arrecife
The capital city of Arrecife is the island's shopping center. The main shopping street is Calle Leon Y Castillo, the locals call the area Calle Real. Bazaars and retail shops sell a variety of goods from clothing to crafts. Prices are very reasonable, and considerably lower than those in major resorts. Many locations accept cash or card.

Biosfera Shopping Center in Puerto del Carmen
Overlooking the Old Town of Puerto del Carmen, this shopping mall is a great destination for clothes. Retailers like Pull and Bear, Levi's, Oyosho, Natural Shop, Crocs, Quicksilver, Pimkie, and Zara can all be found, in addition to an amusement arcade and several bars and restaurants. The mall is located on Calle Juan Carlos I, and is open Monday through Saturday from 10 am to 10 pm, with shortened hours on Sunday.

Deiland Centre in Playa Honda
Another great mall, this indoor shopping center offers a combination of shops, services, and nightlife. Shops selling perfume, clothing, and gifts are all plentiful, as well as a supermarket, a cinema (Spanish only), and a bowling alley. The food court has several restaurants, including KFC and Burger King. Books and media shops make this mall complete.

Old Capital Market in Costa Teguise
Every Sunday morning between 8:30 am and 2 pm, the old capital hosts an outdoor market. Hand-made tablecloths, jewelry, African

Canary Islands Travel Guide

wood carvings, local wines, paintings, and of course, knockoff watches and handbags can all be purchased from local vendors. When you tire of shopping, grab some paella or churros and watch the Canarian dancers in the main square, located in front of the Church. Haggling is expected.

Casa-Museo del Campesino in Mozaga
Most villages throughout the island have shops that sell pottery, basketwork, embroidery, jewelry and other traditional craft items. But the best place to find these items is at the Casa-Museo del Campesino. The museum serves as a monument and tribute to local farmers, and the gift shop is especially known for pottery made using the traditional techniques of hand-carving without a pottery wheel and firing pots in an open fire.

Recommendations for the Budget Traveler to Lanzarote

Printed in Great Britain
by Amazon